T0370504

NAKED

STRIPPING TO THE CORE IN 40 DAYS

Needing Less to Be More

DENA MCMILLON-BILLUPS

AuthorHouse™
1663 Liberty Drive
Bloomington, IN 47403
www.authorhouse.com
Phone: 1 (800) 839-8640

Published by AuthorHouse 08/01/2018

ISBN: 978-1-5462-4520-9 (sc)
ISBN: 978-1-5462-4521-6 (e)

Library of Congress Control Number: 2018906517

Scripture quotations marked KJV are from the Holy Bible, King James Version (Authorized Version). First published in 1611. Quoted from the KJV Classic Reference Bible, Copyright © 1983 by The Zondervan Corporation.

Scripture quotations marked NIV are taken from the Holy Bible, New International Version®. NIV®. Copyright © 1973, 1978, 1984 by International Bible Society. Used by permission of Zondervan. All rights reserved. [Biblica]

Print information available on the last page.

Any people depicted in stock imagery provided by Getty Images are models, and such images are being used for illustrative purposes only. Certain stock imagery © Getty Images.

This book is printed on acid-free paper.

As you explore these meditative exercises, please give yourself permission to answer the questions somewhere on the pages of this book. Doodle your thoughts because your thoughts qualify you to create your day. Partner with me, and please, whatever you do, make sure you own your truth and push toward your creative core.

Introduction

Naked is a forty-day meditation that has contemplative activities following each day. The messages uncover my naked TRUTH and some of the things that have made me feel my most vulnerable.

It's not always easy for me to be vulnerable outside of my intimate circle of loved ones, and when I have been, I've felt insecure and sometimes ashamed. However, I know that I'm covered and clothed by the shadow of God's Word, and that assurance has helped me understand the promises of God, get naked, and uncover the things that would otherwise keep me from breathing and breeding His truth. Stripping to the core has helped me to encourage others as well as seek a deeper meaning for living and refrain from the temptation to just exist.

God has a creative plan for me and for all of us. He is the master creator. The one who needs nothing to create all, He is the one who spoke, "Let there be and it was!" And if God is in us, then what gets in the way of us reaching the incomparable in every area of our lives? Are we operating at our best, from our core: our place of many treasures?

Perhaps it's the images and labels that we portray to others that get in the way of God's plan for us. I don't like to think that I'm much of a label girl, but truth be told, my favorites don't go unnoticed. I have these bling-bad boots that have just the right heel and won't make the feet cry. Oh, but it doesn't stop there; I make sure that I'm wearing my metallic bag that states, "Let me out the front door—my black Harley Davidson is revving up!" When I'm wearing these items, I'm wearing my sass. But what makes the outside look tight and right? Is there a secret to holding it all together?

Okay, I'll let you in on a little secret, and I am not talking about Victoria's Secret. I'm referring to the shapers that we we use to cover and tuck the prime areas, and keep the sass together. You know what I'm talking about—the problem areas. There, I said it. Admitting that I have problem areas doesn't feel right, but I promised God that I would get naked with truth so that we could have the transformation that only happens when we strip to the core.

Even in my best shape, my core could've used a little airbrushing or filtering; this midsection won't let me lie. Of course, I could've pulled off some belly shirts in my earlier days, but as I got older, my battles and experiences added a few pounds that I didn't expect. So, with all that said, the question remains, "Why in the world would anyone want to expose themselves completely naked?" Being naked can feel so intrusive when you fear being judged by others. I know some women will say, "This is me—like it or leave it." But I can't let you stay in that mind-set when the best of us is found at the core.

The core is where the work will take place. The good news is that you have already started the work by beginning this journey with me. My personal trainer taught me that the core, if left unattended, has detrimental effects on the entire body. It's important to strengthen the core and feed yourself the right kinds of foods. It's a system that we can't afford to neglect, because when we do, the level of toxicity defiles the rest of our bodies.

Therefore, I'm challenging you to push toward your creative core—strip the layers off and the labels will fall too.

The labels are many: wife, teacher, daughter, mother, friend, minister, pastor, caregiver, executive, and entrepreneur, just to name a few. Are these labels harmful? Not unless they prevent us from reaching our authentic selves, which is our treasure. It is at the core that we understand our being and the richness of who we are. It's more than just understanding our place of "why." We color the world from our "why," eradicating the norm of black and white to something bold and colorful.

So help me take off these Spanks, work out these challenges, and breath. But first things first: Are you really up for the challenge?

I am challenging you to find your creative core, the place where you can let go and be vulnerable, and begin to lead from there. It's a place far removed from the superficial and external pressures of our culture. It's where we find the urgency to live life by design.

Nonetheless, I am taking a risk by getting naked and undressing this truth. The daily meditations that I will share with you are a snapshot of my nakedness, and as you engage in this journey with me, I ask you to ponder the questions asked of you in the spaces provided, and utilize the blank pages that follow. Please take the time to simply breathe; it's important to sit in that secret place to uncover your truth. The contemplative exercises will help you remove the fat from your life, dig deeper, and discover your creative core. And by digging deeper, you will see the ripples of your muscles unfold at your very core, strengthening you to lead a productive life from where you are.

Leadership is something I think women do naturally without even thinking about it, but often we can't recognize the ability to lead because we are off-centered at our core and have lost our balance in life. When we get into the daily habit of reaching for our core, God will begin to reveal His secret plan to us, which is found at the center of his will and the core of our being. It is through our covenant relationship with the Master Creator that we hear His whisper, and in the midst of a noisy crowd He decodes our touch with words like "Who touched me?" It's in those spoken words that stillness is revealed and captured in the center of chaos.

I'm excited that you've chosen to take this journey with me, and as I was writing this book, I was thinking about the rewards of self-reflective practices. Despite what I've learned about self-reflective practices, I know there is more to discover about the reflectiveness of God. Situations and circumstances are constantly changing, giving us new layers to uncover in the reflective process of change. Remember, it's in this moment that we have and that we share. I thank you for sharing your reflective practices and breakthroughs in advance. You will ultimately be releasing your self-wealth from your creative core on this forty-day journey.

A Sun-Kissed Morning

"I am my beloved and my beloved is mine, he browses among the lilies."

—Song of Songs 6:3

The sun uncovers my nakedness and makes me think of the kiss that's about to happen or the love I'm about to make before the summer ends. I hear my mother say, "You're not grown enough for that kind of love," and before I knew it, I was expecting. But before I can truly embrace what I'm expecting, I have to get excited about the season that I'm in and reach for a love that is kind.

How do you get to a love that is kind? Rise and shine, my dear, and declare your morning. Visualize the sun beaming on you in the warmth of your new day.

Today I declare_____.

Ask yourself this: What did the night leave behind, and what will the dawn of day bring me? Answer this question below.

Are You Expecting?

"Now to him who is able to do immeasurably more than all we ask or imagine, according to his power that is at work within us.""

—Ephesians 3:20, NIV

I haven't always been this ready to conceive, and I know it's kind of invasive of me to ask this of you, but what are you expecting? There are two things we can expect from this life—to live or to die—but either way, we're expecting. If you're not sure what to expect, it's ok. Just remember a pregnant woman isn't ready to deliver her greatness until she reaches her last trimester, so trust the process and be mindful of the fluctuations you'll experience. You will shake the world in due time. In essence, you have to do the same thing as you are going through these reflective practices; allow yourself to feel the fluctuations, as they will be a part of this forty-day journey. More importantly, be intentional and be mindful of the daily details of your life because every experience is a setup for the delivery.

Have you been ignoring the details of your life? Are you able to identify some of the things that keep you from reaching your core? You have to take some risk if you want to get there, but remain watchful for distractions. Are you able to identify the who, what, where, and when of your distractions?

Better yet, quickly bag your distractions for trash day. Oh, how I love trash day! Once a week my garbage truck comes to dispose of the filth; the truck is loud. My dog, Bella, and all the other neighborhood dogs always warn me that the garbage snatcher is near. The clanging and rumbling through the neighborhood is so raucous, but I don't care; I like being on alert that it's time to get rid of the old!

Here it is, imagine your life decluttering; the smelly distractions are leaving, and your garbage lid is lifting, the nasty gnats are being sent back to where they came from—the darkness of the Dumpster. It's important that you understand that your distractions are often your worries that you haven't surrendered.

"Shoo, flies. Don't bother me!" I won't be deceived by your lies.

What are the worries that distract you and fly around your mind like little fruit flies? Write them in the box below.

Who?

What?

Where?

When?

Or Are You Accepting?

"Flesh gives birth to flesh, but the spirit birth to spirit. You should not be surprised at my saying. You must be born again. The wind blows wherever it pleases. You hear its sound, but you cannot tell where it comes from or where it is going. So is with everyone born of the Spirit."

—John 3:6–8

The truth is that if we aren't expecting then we are accepting the lies that rob us of our femininity and dignity. This generation is our future and our promise. We have a responsibility to mentor, to educate, and to protect the gifts that have been given to us. Don't give in to the media-selected hype that has painted this vivid picture of our generation as merely corpses. We who are born of the spirit are called and positioned to live boldly and to speak life to dry bones. Our job is not to battle the monster media but to replace it with the TRUTHS-TRUTHS is an acronym which means Thinking Renewed Under The Holy Spirit. Dry bones are revived with flesh and rise up like an army. Read Ezekiel 37:1–14; my spirit leaps every time I read that passage out loud.

TRUTHS is thinking without limits, which will move our faith beyond what we can think or imagine. The Holy Spirit is fueling our minds with renewed hope, giving us prophetic utterances to speak life over dead situations and circumstances that would dare to keep us in bondage.

Be Open-Minded

So if you're accepting, accept what has already been written. What have you been thinking about lately? What comes out of your mouth is always a telltale sign to the operation of your mind or what you choose to believe and act on today.

TRUTHS activates the mind to ART—Activate Right Thinking. And ART gives us movement. I love this passage below; it's how we discern truth and receive renewed hope:

> The messiah will suffer and rise from the dead on the third day, and repentance for the forgiveness of sins will be preached in His name to all nation beginning at Jerusalem. You are witnesses of these things. I am going to send you what my Father has promised; but stay in the city until you have been clothed with power from on high. (Luke 2:46–47)

Stripping

Go back to the passage in Luke and circle the words that stand out for you. Do you believe this passage for your life? Why or why not? What is the operative motive in your mind when you read this passage?

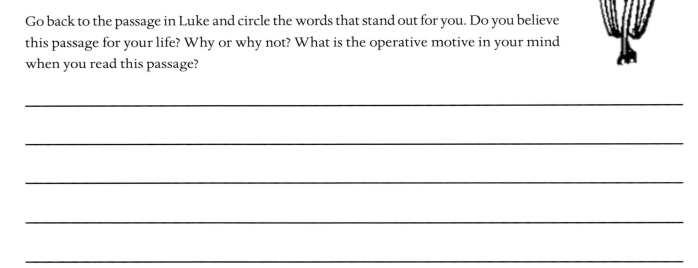

_____

_____

_____

_____

What Will the Truth Do for You?

"Then I passed by and saw you kicking about in your blood, and as you lay there in your blood I said to you, "Live!" I made you grow like a plant of the field. You grew and developed and entered puberty. Your breasts had formed and your hair had grown; yet you were stark naked. Later I passed by you and saw you, and behold, you were at the time for love; so I spread My skirt over you and covered your nakedness."

—Ezekiel 16:6–7

TRUTHS will make you feel safe when you've been exposed. It's your gift in the process of your nakedness and in the vulnerable areas of your life. But as with any gift, you have to unwrap it. TRUTHS will speak to all who are born with a God conscious. We are made in His image, and when we don't see Him, we yearn for His presence to fill us. Do we go about kicking in our blood when our needs are unmet? It's your free will to accept this truth or not. I'm the first to admit that I need the presence of our Abba Father and the love of His Spirit breathing through me, hovering over me, and covering me with the fabric of His beauty. So I don't mind getting naked, for He sees me and saves me from dying in my naked imperfections.

Do you understand the patterns of fabric that cover you in your life? What is your thread count? How are you designed? Whatever has been weaved through you and whatever is connected to you creates a pattern that expresses your mood, attitude, and personality.

Fill in the pieces of your fabric below.

What are you made of?

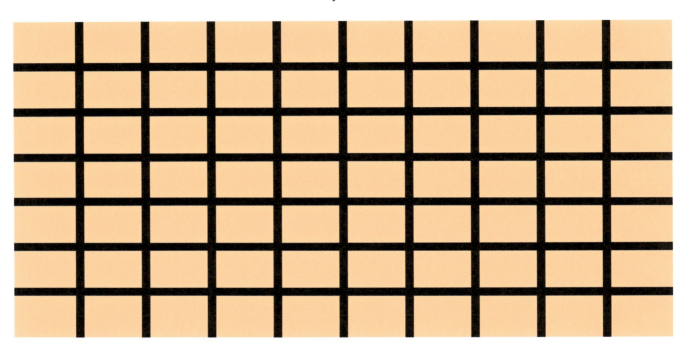

Ready for a Makeover?

"I praise you because I am fearfully and wonderfully made your works are wonderful, I know that full well."

—Psalm 139:14

Wonderfully Made

Although I dabble in the makeup industry, my daughter is the makeup artist. It empowers us to see women get good makeovers, especially the women who say, "I don't wear makeup," or "My boyfriend or husband doesn't like when I wear makeup." Although those statements annoy me, I understand risk and change. People are afraid of change or what others will think if they make the change. Sometimes people are afraid that the makeup will show them up. And trust me, that should never happen. You wear makeup; makeup should never, ever, wear you. A good makeup artist is aware of this and will secretly chuckle at your resistance. Needless to say, my daughter has done some serious miracle transformations just from using a good foundation brush and a little contouring.

Spiritual Makeovers

Spiritual makeovers manifest good makeovers, too, as you expect, accept, and expand your thinking. Let God lay the foundation for your makeover, and be intentional, take the initiative, and connect with your own creative muse. First, beware if you are not invested in the makeover process and cannot trust God the artist—you will only feel and look like a clown at the end of the makeover.

You deserve the desired change, but take the time and do it for yourself. I'd hate for someone to tell you that you need a makeover—ouch, that hurts! As you connect and spend time with the lover of your soul, God will contour those imperfections and provide for you the right coverage for being fearfully and wonderfully made.

I know that the brush of His spirit will shape you and quench your God conscious into something beautiful. Today, expect something new and beautiful—you!

If you could contour one thing in your life, what would that be?

The one thing I would contour in my life is _____.

I'm Good

For the many women who say, "No, I'm good--I don't need a makeover." Take a look at my friends in this scenario, please help me decide which one is good: Goodgirl or Girlgood?

Girlgood is at work and notices that Goodgirl is acting differently toward her. Girlgood believes it may be because of her recent promotion and thinks that Goodgirl is acting jealous. Both girls used to have working lunches together and worked very hard to collaborate on notable accomplishments. After a staff meeting, Girlgood asked if Goodgirl wanted to meet for lunch and the answer Goodgirl gave was an abrupt no. Girlgood was very disappointed and hurt because she has been so good to the Goodgirl and recently supported her through a family crisis.

Goodgirl was very excited about Girlgood's recent promotion and did not go to lunch with her because she wanted to meet with other members of their team to plan a celebration for Girlgood's success. Now Goodgirl is starting to think that perhaps the recent promotion is going to Girlgood's head and decides

to keep her distance from her. Goodgirl was so excited about the good news she had to share with Girlgood, but forget about it; Girlgood will have to wait to hear about the news. Girlgood doesn't know that she will be rewarded at the next staff meeting for her publications and hard work.

Because of Girlgood's recent behavior, Goodgirl has refocused and has also become distant. Goodgirl believes that if it weren't for her going out of her way to help Girlgood, she wouldn't have gotten the promotions in the first place.

Challenge Question

Which girl is good? Goodgirl or Girlgood? A little confused? Well, Proverbs 21:2 sums it up perfectly. Every man's way is right in his own eyes, but the Lord weighs the heart. And Isaiah 64:6 makes it plain that all of us have become like one who is unclean, and all our righteous acts are like filthy rags; we shrivel up like a leaf, and like the wind our sins sweep us away. Let's take a closer look.

Who's in the mirror?

Does she look familiar to you?

What's her story, and how different is she than you?

Is she different?

Has her heart ached like yours?

Is she living, or is she dying?

Is she pretty, or is she ugly? Is she pretending, or is she mending? Is it about her needs, or is it about yours?

Who's in the mirror?

Goodgirl or Girlgood?

Get Your Makeup Wipes Ready

"Therefore, having put away falsehood let each one of you speak the truth with his neighbor, for we are members one of another."

—Ephesians 4:25

Are you still having trouble with the truth? Let's get the makeup wipes ready. Isn't it easier to hide from the truth when you're wearing cover up. The truth can make us feel vulnerable while exposing our insecurities to ourselves and others. Now, I'm not suggesting that wisdom be left out when sharing personal information with others, but I am suggesting that we take a closer look at what we're communicating to the world. Get ready, because the blemishes are real, and what you take off becomes the truth you work with. Let's take a closer look.

Pray and ask God to reveal to you who your confidant will be. We all need someone to keep us accountable and honest. I'm concerned about people who don't have someone who will keep them honest. If you're not used to hearing what others have to say about you, it may be difficult at first. You may even become offended, so please do this next activity with someone you respect and trust.

A Close Up

Get the makeup wipes ready. Ask yourself these questions. Are you a woman of integrity? Do you keep your commitments to yourself and others? Are you ready to release the drama from your life? Are you afraid of letting go? Are you willing to seek help for change? Is change something you are prepared to pursue on your own? What are you willing to wipe off in exchange for truth?

Draw a line down the middle in the space provided. On the left side of the line should be the questions you answer about yourself, and on the right side of the line should be the questions you and your confidant answer together. Be ready to write about what you learn about yourself during this exercise?

Make Me Over

"For behold, I create new heavens and a new earth; and the former things will not be remembered or come to mind."

—Isaiah 65:17

Make over.

Make me over; I can't see me!

Make me over; I can't be me!

I look in the mirror, and I'm horrified by me.

Someone remove this makeup,

Because I don't know me.

Never mind; give me back my cover up

Because the smudges from my tears

Won't shut up.

Where's my concealer, because the wrinkles of pride

Keep showing up.

Airbrush the lines of lust because every now and then I still get that rush.

Makeover these dark circles; my reputation is on the line.

Color my cheekbones; my low self-esteem won't leave me alone.

I keep changing my lip gloss, hoping that these negative words won't cost.

So make me over; I can't be me. I look in the mirror, and I'm horrified by me.

This cosmetic regimen has taken over the beauty in me.

Make me over.

This foundation is all wrong; I can't see me.

My God, my God, please break me,

So I can see your image in me.

I surrender me.

Please transform this beauty in me.

> Are you ready to exchange your beauty regimen for your heavenly Father's? Even His feet are beautiful. Isaiah 52:7 tells us how beautiful on the mountains are the feet of those who bring good news, who proclaim peace, who bring good tidings, who proclaim salvation, who say to Zion, "Your God reigns!"
>
> "To appoint unto them that mourning Zion. To give unto them beauty for ashes, the oil. joy for mourning, the garment of praise for the spirit of heaviness, that the night be called trees of righteousness, the planting of the Lord, that He may be glorified. ."
>
> Isaiah 61:3

Take out your mirror again—who is she? Have you ever met Grace? She is your beauty reflection, and she is defined through the redemption that came by Christ Jesus. Do you see her in the mirror? If yes, describe her below. If you cannot find Grace in the mirror than describe what you think she might look like.

His Gift to You

"I will ask the father and he will give you another counselor to be with you forever."

—John 14:16

It is pride that must be broken so that we can respond to our naked truth. It is the Holy Spirit that applies the truth to our inner beings, guiding us to a road of resolve. The Holy Spirit comes with sweet counsel to our hearts and minds, and when we respond to this conviction that we cannot save ourselves from ourselves, then we surrender. We surrender our brokenness, which frees us of all guilt and shame.

The gift of salvation is not forced upon us because our God is too much of a gentleman for that. I just wish that I had been as gentle with myself over the years as God has been with me, and I wish I hadn't waited so long to forgive myself. I don't know if it started somewhere in childhood, but I remember being so unforgiving of myself when I'd fall off the bumpy trails of life.

Bike riding is so fun and freeing for me; it brings back so many memories from grade school years with my best friend Felicia. We'd bike ride through the hill and trails of the "7-11 Mountain," as we called it, and I could always count on Felicia to be by my side, ready to rescue me from the falls. I was so tickled and yet a little disappointed when I discovered what I thought was a mountain was in fact a very small hill. It's now hysterical to see that the mountain-hill was not as intimidating as I had conjured up in my mind, and maybe that's why it was so easy for Felicia to hurdle to the other side and help me. Things always appear bigger when you're younger, and the mountains I used to have to climb are so small. Most of what we perceive has to do with where we are developmentally in life. During that time, I perceived falling down as something I deserved, so it was easy to accept the pain that came with the falls. Some of the mountains in my life didn't even exist. But in a best friend kind of way, Felicia knew I was struggling, and she would grab my hand and pull me up so that we could enjoy the rest of the ride together. So too does the Holy Spirit help us up and down the hills of life, ready to guide us back on the right path and over the mountains we struggle to climb.

I didn't realize that getting up from the fall and getting back on the ride of life would bring so much assurance. It's as if the breeze that I felt through my thick ponytails connected me to my forward motion, peddling to the end of the trails. The freedom and the speed of wind releases the pain once experienced from the fall.

Who will save you from the fall, the hills we climb in this life? Who will counsel you when you hit the bottom and struggle on your own to get up? Who will ease the pain and apply truth during some of the toughest hills you will ever climb? Will you ride alone?

Who's riding with you?

God is a strategic trailblazer; He will send your biker buddies on the trail when it's too challenging to go on alone. Who are your biker buddies, your "ride or die?" I call them my ride-or-die buddies-- culturally it means that they are going to be with you through the tough times; they're your village. Whose hand will you grab at the bottom of the hill? It's important that we identify them by name, and more important that we nurture those relationships. Your riding buddies are on assignment for your life. Although there is no guarantee they will be with you always, they are the ones who you can call two o'clock in the morning. They will rise with you and meet you where you are. I have lost four riding buddies, Kiera, Adrienne, Bonita, and Marie, so I know how important it is to never take your ride-or-die buddies for granted. You never know when it will be time to say good-bye.

My heart still grieves, you were too young to leave us behind, and I miss you all so deeply. We helped each other when we took falls in life. I have no regrets about the time I spent with you—I just wish we had more time to ride.

List your ride-or-die buddies below, reach out to them and make sure you set up quality face time. They are your lifelines, and they have a purpose that will create new trails and paths for you to travel.

The Developmental Stages Mature You

"For everyone who lives on milk is unskilled in the word of righteousness, since he is a spiritual infant. But solid food is for the mature; whose senses are trained by practice to distinguish between what is morally good and what is evil."

— Hebrews 5:13–14

Through the developmental stages of life, we are doing these three things: stopping, slowing down, or moving forward. What's frustrating for me is not that women aren't trying to live purposeful lives, but that the media and reality TV shows have portrayed them as backstabbing, backbiting, sexually desperate, needy, and every woman out for herself, which means to me there is a failure to thrive. I know that the term *failure to thrive* is often used in the field of child welfare when there have been signs of abuse and neglect. Sometimes doctors may notice a child whose current development or weight is much lower than that of other children of the same age. Medical factors and environmental factors are considered, and development is in question.

If there's a failure to thrive, then who's stunting your growth? Perhaps you want to grow, but there are people who rather not see you climb the growth chart of life. Is your environment unhealthy? Is abuse or neglect a factor? If so, how? I still clutch my pearls when I hear women call one another everything but the birth name given by their mothers. It pains me when jealousy arises between women, and I'm not afraid to cut this topic at the root. I challenge women with my motto "I am her and she is me" when they say I don't need girlfriends. I find that to be the excuse and the need to be just the opposite. I challenge you to spit out the bitterroot and ask yourself this question: "Would I want to be my own girlfriend?" Are you someone who others want to communicate with?

So who is she? She is I, my sister! I have these sisters that I call my fab-five—I prayed them into my life. My prayer went something like this: "God, please send me new friends that love You, have a vision and purpose for life, and are kind of cool and sassy like me!" But seriously, I believe God not only sent me these women, but that they were the bonus that came with the job I prayed for about ten years ago. Initially when I started that job, I felt so suffocated by the cubicle culture (which is another topic in itself) that I forgot I had prayed for cool and sassy girlfriends and began to complain the first day. I turned up my nose and under my breath I uttered, "I'm good; I don't need any new friends near my cubicle." Thank my Lord and Savior—He can ignore a fickle utterance when He hears one, because these women have changed my life!

We prayed for one another's lives, that spiritual and natural gifts would manifest, and that our children and families would be blessed. We prayed through the struggles of singlehood, and we kept one another accountable even when we didn't want to. There was this little lunch spot that we called the upper room; there we would not only have lunch but communion prayer. Let's just say we were radicals for living lives filled with purpose. At that time we were all single, but after prayer and sometimes fasting, we all got married within five years of one another. Visions came to fruition, nonprofit organizations were formed, and graduate degrees were accomplished. We had great vision parties and mission trips to Africa. We became authors, artists, prayer intercessors, educators, and huge risk takers by faith. These women were my accountability partners at their finest, and even if we didn't always agree with one another we were able to respect the position we had in one another's life. It's a part of the getting naked with TRUTH, even at the risk of losing a relationship. There were times when we had to say, "no" or agree to disagree with one another, so that we could push one another in an authentic way towards our self-wealth. You have to be ready to receive sassy and cool women in your life, but everything comes at a cost. No relationship is maintenance free, and we had to be mindful to pray for one another. Although we are all married now, we know how to show up in one another's lives when a crisis breaks out or just because we need we time. I'm so rich because of the developmental stages of these relationships and how they have grown.

Where are your relationships developmentally? Do you need to nurture those relationships or perhaps welcome new ones? Is there a failure to thrive in your old ones? I'm convinced that all of God's people are sassy and cool when living out their purpose, and I believe God's networking system in motion will blow your mind.

I have seen God do amazing things and rekindle old relationships too. I ran into an old friend in a store, and we promised each other coffee for one year, once a week, before the husbands and the miracle babies came. How wonderful it was to see us grow through the reflective process of laughter, tears, and desired hope for the future. I couldn't put a price on the tea and coffee conversations with Tonia—they were more than divine, they were liberating.

Proverbs 18:24 states, "a man that has friends must show himself friendly, and there is a friend that sticketh closer than a brother." I challenge you to be the sassy sister who knows her self-wealth and strips to the core as she discovers her relationships with herself and others.

Don't be stingy; invest your time and talent into someone's life in a way that edifies that person.

Are your relationships growing the way you need them too? What could you do more of and what could you do less of? Take some time to do ART—Activate Right Thinking—below by drawing symbols or sketches of some ideas on how you could give to a friend today or a sister who is need of a friend.

There Is an End that Begins

―――∞―――

"For surely there is an end; and thine expectation shall not be cut off."

— Proverbs 23:18

There is a reward for those who earnestly seek the Lord; however, if you're not expecting, please don't get offended by my creative expression to speak boldly, live boldly, and share my vulnerabilities, hopes, and dreams. I hope that through some of my poetic writings and illustrations we can thread through the commonalities that keep us expecting. God's Word is the seed that impregnates us with TRUTHS. When we're open to responding by faith, we push from the core toward God's manifested greatness. If you're moving forward, then going back aborts the plan.

I discovered years ago that God gives us gifts that are for His use, and to activate those gifts, you have to be close to the activator. I spent a lot of my years fueling my mind with "I should" thoughts, and I know if I reached back to my early childhood days, I'd find the recording of " I should" in my household, church community, and even school, so no it's not surprising that I often got stuck on "I should" or "you should" recordings and often felt the temptations to live my life swimming within those confines.

"I should" color inside the lines, but if I followed that rule I would have expected to live in the shackles of the status quo. So today, if you have a yearning to go deeper with me and to be true to who you are at the core, then together we can explore. Of course, it's easier to just fit into the bubble of the norm, and it's harder to push when you're not feeling pregnant. So let's stay focused on the idea that you are expecting. Shout out loud, "I'm expecting!"

If I pick up a pencil, I expect to create in Him. If I speak, I expect to be His mouthpiece with rivers of living water gushing out. If I pick up a paintbrush, I expect to cover His canvas with explosive oils. If I write, I expect that He is the ghostwriter of the story. If I dance, I expect that music will be played from the angels' harps.

Living in expectation leaves you with the giddy feeling of a young girl in love. But it's not enough to just flirt with the truth; there is a magic that happens when you make a conscious commitment to hold fast to God's truth by His design.

How do you manage your gifts? Have you opened your hands to release what has freely been given to you? And I am not talking about just being a good helper; most women have an innate ability to do that. We move quickly to help those who are important to us. My sweetest Edna raised something like $5,000 in two days for her daughter to go to Africa. Afterward we talked about how we needed that same urgency for ourselves when God shows us a plan for our own lives. Seriously, if you could have seen this mother's love in action, it was faith incredible!

But how do we create that same kind of urgency for action in our own lives? Does God love us so much more than we could love our families? Why do we put everyone else above the eternal whispers and messages that God has for us? Can you tell me what's urgent for you?

Fro Rock the Car Lot?

"For I know the plans I have for you, declares the lord, plans to prosper you and not harm you, plans to give hope and a future."

— Jeremiah 29:11

It had been more than six months since I left my full-time job with a passion to fulfill my purpose and the resiliency to survive the loss of what once was a comfortable nine to five. My urgency plan was in operative slow mode. I had started a coaching business before I left my job with all good intentions to coach, speak, and do training for individuals and organizations looking for creative change, and I too was ready for change, but I wasn't sure if change had accepted its calling for me. Finally, after hitting the pavement networking, soliciting leads and connections, I ran into the tunnel of financial halt. Looking for new ways to do work differently, as my therapist described it. Yes, therapist— do you actually think leaving my job after ten years was easy? No!

Honey, I tied up some aromatherapy sessions and good forty-five-minute talks, which felt like I was having a conversation with a girlfriend who sparked me to rest, relax, and color outside the lines again in the pursuit of change and because my health depended on it. I was trying to find my swag again, live life without regrets, and I wasn't going back at any cost. In fact, I told people I would do whatever it took to pursue what I believed God was calling me to, even if it meant interviewing for a car sales position; I had never sold cars before, but I was on a mission. My business was still in the very early stages, and I needed a concurrent plan and decided that selling cars could be a temporary solution to my current household needs. Of course, there were people spreading gossip like fake news. They were smiling while shaking their heads and whispering, "What is she doing now?" They bought their friends' doubt and fear and watched on the sidelines. Would that surprise you? Whenever you are entering unfamiliar territory, you have to protect your process from the naysayers.

What about you? Is it just me or have you ever tried to make your plan God's plan? If you answered yes, tell me who showed up at your sidelines? Did fear show up? How did you respond to the fake news?

Shower Eyes

—❦—

"Before they call I will answer; while they are still speaking I will hear."

—Isaiah 65:24

The morning seemed cruel from the start. I wasn't sure if it was the water from the shower that ran down my cheeks or my own tears, but God and I had a quick conversation, and it went like this: "God, I don't really want this job, but I don't want to let my family down. I will go on the interview, but I believe in my heart this is not what You would have for me. I don't understand Your timing, and I thought we worked this out already."

As I was getting ready for the interview, I could not find my right shoe, and to top it off, as I rushed passed the mirror, I was horrified by the grays that decided they wanted to go on the interview with me because I had no time to cover them up. My heart was racing when I realized the time; I had only a half an hour left to get to the interview. My daughter walked past me in the bathroom and said, "Mom! Mom! What's wrong? You have to get it together! You look fine!"

Sobbing, I said, "I can't find my shoe, and I have to gooooooooo!"

She said, "Mom, breathe. Pull it together. Put your makeup on and pull back your hair; you look fine, just go!"

My husband was working from home that day and said, "Dena, do you want the job? Don't go if you don't want it."

I answered, "I can't find my shoe." How ironic was it that I couldn't find my right shoe? Right?

I sobbed the entire way to the interview. On my way there, I called my mother to apologize for burdening her with my right shoe problem and my interview meltdown. She responded, "Dena, I understand what your week has been like; stop apologizing. You are my only daughter, and I am here for you." I found comfort in her words, and I had enough time to make one more phone call before I arrived at my destination. I had to call the daycare where our little lion king attended to let them know he wasn't coming in that day. As I was about to hang up the call, the director asked if I was okay and if I wanted to pray. It was quick, but powerful. God will always send His light into the darkest places if you will allow and receive. The director was a good friend of mine, and she could sense my interview meltdown voice.

My Pastor once asked, "have you ever been in the wrong place at the right time?" That question came to my mind again on my way to the interview. I knew that looking at where I was wasn't the focus—I had to change the way I thought about where I was and where I was going. Have you ever gone to the wrong place at the right time? Maybe you're at that particular place now. As believers, we stand on the promises of Roman 8:28, and we know that in all things God works for the good of those who love Him, who have been called according to His purpose.

What has the wrong place at the right time looked like for you? Please take the time to sketch what that looks like below.

Where's My Greater?

———— ❦ ————

"Very truly I tell you, whoever believes in me will do the works I have been doing, and they will do even greater things than these, because I am going to the Father."

—John 14:12

I knew I was a complete mess when I arrived at the interview. Where had this freeway really taken me? "Hello," I said. "I'm here for the interview to speak with the person who's supposed to interview me." Who says that? I had no time to get embarrassed about forgetting the interviewer's name; I was so unprepared and was hoping no one would look down and notice my combat boots with my interview dress. I never found that right shoe, but I think I was in the wrong place at the right time. There was a lesson in this, and now I just had to figure out what that lesson was. It's so important to be mindful of our moments so that we don't miss out on the right shoe.

Where's the right shoe?

I waited for the manager for two hours, and then the manager had only three questions for me. The first question he asked was, "Why do you want to be a car salesperson?" I wanted to answer that I didn't, but instead I said, "Well, I believe we sell ourselves daily, and besides, I know my leadership, training, and engagement skills are transferable." He looked at me, and I guess he liked the answer because he proceeded to his next question, which in retrospect was not only inappropriate but borderline unlawful. I answered yes to the question of having children, and that's when he showed me the 9:00 a.m. to 9:00 p.m. schedule I would have if I wanted the job there. Lastly, he mentioned that all the cars sales personnel worked on 100 percent commission and asked if I still wanted the position? My pause was probably longer than the time he spent interviewing me, and I said, "I don't think I am a good fit for this job." He thanked me for my honesty and the interview ended with a handshake and smile. I marched out the door with my combat boots as if I had won the interview meltdown war. I was still trying to quiet my soul on the ride home, and as it got quiet, I felt God speaking. "Have you asked Me for what you want?"

Then I began to pray, "God, I want to use the gifts that You have given me freely."

I heard, "Well, open your hands."

I got it! Our gifts are for releasing, and as long as I had kept my hands closed, it would be hard to receive the benefits that God had for me. As I arrived home, I still felt upset that I had wasted so much time, but my spirit had quickened because time was not wasted in learning the lesson. I had stripped a layer off with this experience, and I was getting closer to the core. If I could be tempted to work a 9:00 a.m. to 9:00 p.m. job outside of my purpose on a 100 percent commission, then what would stop me from doing my own business, my purpose? It wasn't until I took the freeway to that interview that I realized I had left my job but not changed my thinking. I had integrated cubicle thinking into managing my new work life. I had not learned to value my self-wealth. If only I could trust God through this process and His compensation plan for me. Did I deny myself access to the principle of reaping and sowing?

It was time to open my hands. God had already blessed me with the compensation plan; I just had to be ready to work the plan. Today I open my hands to release my art, my ministry, and my businesses and sow them into the life of others. This stretching of the faith is not for the faint of heart. I've learned some valuable lessons from those salesmen and -women in the dealership that day. They were working long hours and expecting a payoff. They trusted the process as they put their time in. They expected a great return: a commission check that would compensate for all of the hours they worked.

Commission is a sum of money that is paid to an employee upon completion of a task.

The commission is the incentive to get the employee to do something. I believe that God has an incentive plan for us, and there is a commission for those who labor in their gifts. You will see a return if you are diligent in the process, but it hurts sometimes. We have to put in the hours and count up the cost, even when others around you aren't invested in the process.

Meditate on Matthew 25:14–30 below, and tell me how it speaks to your heart and how it activates right thinking in your life. What will you do with your talents?

> For it will be like a man going on a journey, who called his servants and entrusted to them his property. To one he gave five talents, to another two, to another one, to each according to his ability. Then he went away. He who had received the five talents went at once and traded with them, and he made five talents more. So also he who had the two talents made two talents more. But he who had received the one talent went and dug in the ground and hid his master's money. Now after a long time the master of those servants came and settled accounts with them. And he who had received the five talents came forward, bringing five talents more, saying, "Master, you delivered to me five talents; here, I have made five talents more." His master said to him, "Well done, good and faithful servant. You have been faithful over a little; I will set you over much. Enter into the joy of your master." And he also who had the two talents came forward, saying, "Master, you delivered to me two talents; here, I have made two talents more." His master said to him, "Well done, good and faithful servant. You have been faithful over a little; I will set you over much. Enter into the joy of your master." He also who had received the one talent came forward, saying, "Master, I knew you to be a hard man, reaping where you did not sow, and gathering where you scattered no seed, so I was afraid, and I went and hid your talent in the ground. Here, you have what is yours." But his master answered him, "You wicked and slothful servant! You knew that I reap where I have not sown and gather where I scattered no seed? Then you ought to have invested my money with the bankers, and at my coming I should have received what was my own with interest. So take the talent from him and give it to him who has the ten talents. For to everyone who has will more be given, and he will have an abundance. But from the one who has not, even what he has will be taken away And cast the worthless servant into the outer darkness. In that place there will be weeping and gnashing of teeth."

The Power of Expectation

"For surely there is an end and thine expectation shall not be cut off."

—Proverbs 23:18

We are required to live in the power of expectations, and when we surrender to the fact that the Lord is our shepherd daily: movement happens. My journey on the freeway was neither the first nor the last, but the difference is I'm now learning how to declare what I expect through Christ. As you start this day, start with the expectation that you are moving forward going from glory to glory. Our entire Christian life can be summed up by the redemption, sanctification, and freedom that makes all things new on earth to that glorious day where the Lord will say, "Well done, my good and faithful servant." Because of the complacency we put on ourselves when we neglect the power of expectation, I'd like to share one of my favorite worship songs with you, "Moving Forward" by Israel Houghton. It's in my daily practice and quiet space that I find time to be where the King dwells. In that time and space, I play love songs to the Most High; it decreases my anxiety about the unknown and positions me in the certainty that God is a God of movement. It is here that plans become strategic because truth becomes relevant in light of our identity in Christ. In this place, It will be beneficial for you to download this song today and listen intently to the words as you envision yourself moving forward, and not turning back. Please see old doors shut and new ones open as you live in the expectant possibilities. Enjoy your worship!

Possibilities

"And looking at them Jesus said to them; 'With people this is impossible, but with God all things are possible.'"

—Matthew 19:26

Are you ready to make this day come alive with possibilities? I've chosen Eve from the book of Genesis to help you discover your roots and get a close-up of nature versus nurture. The contrast of her story and the readiness of my pen motivate me to uncover the pain and make right the secrets of the heart. While I know that God will be with us, I'm on assignment to ink the naked truth of who we are on this laborious journey to push. Choose your possibilities wisely; one of Eve's possibilities shamed her, exposing her nakedness.

Be mindful of this day, because it's in this day that tomorrow will be affected—it will impact your week, your month, and your year. As you surrender to this thought, you will find that each day has its own rhythm that is dimmed by the moon or lit by the sun. Today we make our choice to be in the light or stand in the shadows. At the end of this day, I want you to draw the possibilities of your day on the next page. If something was made possible for you today, illustrate what that looks like. I'm not asking you to be an artist; I'm asking you to allow the art in you to be. What did the possibility of gratitude look like for you today? Did it have you dancing? Today, I'm facing some obstacles. Although the doors are closed behind me, I'm thankful for this opportunity to share and open something in this moment. I'm surrendering my fear in exchange for who I was created to be. I'm created to be creative, and I release the entangled thoughts and receive the abundance of something greater than what I see in front of me. Sometimes the reflection of possibility scares me, so forgive me if this picture isn't perfect. How would draw your possibility reflection?

The Real Housewife of Eden

"Then the Lord God said, 'It is not good for the man to be alone; I will make him a helper suitable for him.'"

Genesis 2:18

Before we push and birth what God has for us today, let's confront the "real housewife of Eden." Can we have a little fun?

The real housewife was the housewife of Eden. Of course, Eve had her issues, yet, she became the giver of life. Is life achieved through a birthing process? Who gives us that right? Birthing happens, either through a physical manifestation or conceptual idea, and a woman has been chosen to birth life. A chosen vessel of God according to the book of Genesis, she's the mother of all humanity.

What has God called you to birth? Are you a giver or a taker of life? Did Eve have a problem listening to her Father? Did her daddy issues cause her to fall and bite off more than she could chew? What would the Real Housewife of Eden say happened? Perhaps, "Sorry my senses happen to be off." Be mindful and aware of your five senses so that you do not sit in human error or poison deceit.

Take two minutes to quiet everything around you. Focus completely on the apple and time this activity for two minutes. When your two minutes are up, please write down your thoughts. What were you thinking, during this activity? What was the strongest of your five senses? Was your focus off? Were you able to quiet the noise? Why or why not?

DAY 17

That Girl

⁓⁓⁓

"The Lord god planted a garden toward the east, in Eden; and there He placed the man whom He had formed."

—Genesis 2:8

Her husband has given her the code for the tree of life, and he unlocks it by hanging out with God in the cool of the day. Eve is "that girl"; her life is like a dream that most of us wish was our reality. Her mate is strong, and he names the world as he sees it. She owns her nakedness and lived her life until things got complicated.

Eve was on top of the world with a zeal for life until the fall.

There's always going to be someone we admire or wish our lives replicated. Things seem so easy for the people you admire when you're looking from the outside, until you see them fall. I'll admit I'm a people watcher; I used to sit with my daughter at the mall when she was a little girl, and we'd tell stories about what we thought someone's life was like. It was like entertainment without the cost of expensive popcorn and soft drinks. Isn't it easier to imagine yourself in someone else's life on those days when you struggle to look at your own?

That's why reality TV has high ratings—so many people are interested in looking into the windows of others. It just seems easier to escape through someone else's drama instead of facing your own. We know that in life disappointment is inevitable, and sooner or later we will all face our own reality and sudden falls.

If Eve had her own reality show, we would all be glued to the tube because our lives depended on hers. We would be watching to see her next move, her choices, and the climactic moment of how she was going to escape the tempter and the decision to be seduced by the infamous forbidden fruit. Would we change the channel at that moment, or would we watch to see the manifestation of the fall? Nevertheless, her story is our reality; we face the juicy temptations of the seducing voices of our culture daily, despite the consequences of what we might face as a result. Do we still face this reality of the first woman who genetically connects us to our sin nature, or has God's promises and nurturing love for us given us a second chance at an Eden environment? Do our external existences based on receiving a second Adam determine rather we choose to live or die?

When I lost my very close friend to suicide, I was devastated. I could tell you her story, but I won't. It's too close to mine. So I will speak louder than your thoughts or the temptations to give up or give in, because I know the illusionist wants to deceive you. He wants to keep you from taking daily inventory, which I know too well. I know the heat and the fire of what deception looks and feels like; therefore, I know not to trust myself or my desires. I have to be intentional in doing a mind inventory check, during which I take my thoughts captive.

The following scriptures support me in the renewing of my mind and my mind inventory check:

> "We demolish arguments and every pretension that sets itself up against the knowledge of God, and we take captive every thought to make it obedient to Christ."
>
> —2 Corinthians 10:5
>
> "Put to death therefore what is earthly in you: sexual immorality, impurity, passion, evil desire, and covetousness, which is idolatry."
>
> —Colossians 3:5
>
> "Focus your mind today on whatsoever things are true, whatsoever things are pure, whatsoever things are lovely, whatsoever things are of good report, if there be any virtue and if there be any praise, think on these things."
>
> —Philippians 4:8

It is most natural to have the sin nature, that principle that makes us rebellious against God. It's not in our nakedness that we die; it's in our nakedness that we live and show ourselves to the one who created and knows our imperfections, doubts, insecurities, fears, and delusional thoughts. It's in our nakedness that we should be unashamed of our image, because we were fearfully and wonderfully made in His image. In God we are nurtured to our true nature, and it's at the center of our core that we find we are made perfect in Him who cultivates who we are.

Let's Get Naked

In what manner or attitude do you approach God?

Here are some practical ways that I found most helpful in approaching God. You may find a different way that works better for your life. But these can be helpful in finding peace when drama is present.

1. Be Still

    In the morning, practice being still. Take five minutes to not do anything but quiet your soul. Try not to turn on any devices. When you hear the surrounding noise going away, that means you are becoming more focused. I like to get up earlier than everyone else, which helps eliminate distractions.

2. Pray

    When we wait to pray, it shows that we reverence God. Sometimes my most effective prayers were the simple ones when I just said, "Jesus, please help me when I can't help myself." I believe it's because He is looking at the heart of our prayers, not the length. That prayer is so impactful in my life, and more importantly it helps me to realize that I am nothing without Him and everything with Him.

3. Let God Speak

    What is God saying to you specifically? Get in the practice of asking that question so that you will become more familiar with His voice. Write it down so you can understand His dialogue with you and hold up what you hear with the truth, the biblical principles of His Word.

4. Apply TRUTHS

    Applying the truth will keep you living a purposeful life according to the core of who you are called to be and from a place of self-wealth.

Having It All Isn't Everything

⟡

"When the woman saw that the fruit of the tree was good for food and pleasing to the eye, and also desirable for gaining wisdom, she took some and ate it. She also gave some to her husband who was with her, and he ate it."

—Genesis 3:6

Did she expect to live, or did she expect to die? What was her reality, and how did she fall from grace? Will somebody please tell me when the drama began and when did it end? How did things turn for the worse? When did she lose her zeal? When did she step out of position? It's in the book of Genesis that we began to understand her struggle and ours, in the role of first lady, and the "real housewife of Eden." Eve wanted what she wanted. It was not a foreign concept for Eve to have it all, but did Eve know what to expect? What was barren in the hollow part of her soul? It appears her soul could not get quieted; as a result, she chased after the forbidden and fell beneath God's will for her life. Are you chasing the forbidden?

I wish she would have known the power of her influence and that she was the mother of the living. You too can influence an entire generation, but how will you use your influence? Where is your focus? Where's your creative core, your center, your self-wealth?

Who are the people you encounter on a daily basis? How do they impact your center focus?

Let's assess your life domains and focus on how each domain impacts you as an individual. What are the risk factors and protective factors in each category that keep you balanced and centered? Below is a life-coaching tool that I've used myself and with my coaching clients. According to Noomii.com, this is "The Ultimate Wheel of Life Interactive Assessment" used by a network of life coaches. It is a simple but powerful tool that helps you visualize your life at a glance through several domains. This visual tool will help you gain focus on areas of your life where there is a need for improvement.

Are you ready to take inventory and asses your truth? Then read the instructions on the next page and create your own personalized interactive Wheel Assessment.

The Wheel Assessment is for you to assess different aspects of your life. Each domain is numbered from 1 to 10, shade in the domain areas with 10 being the most satisfied. Once you've completed the areas on the wheel ask God to develop a plan for the areas you want to improve. As a life coach I have worked with many clients using this wheel, and I usually offer this tool in our first session together. See yourself at the center of the wheel with your core values at the forefront. This is my bonus resource to help you strip to the core, also you may sign up for a free consultation when you register on my website www.denabillups.com.

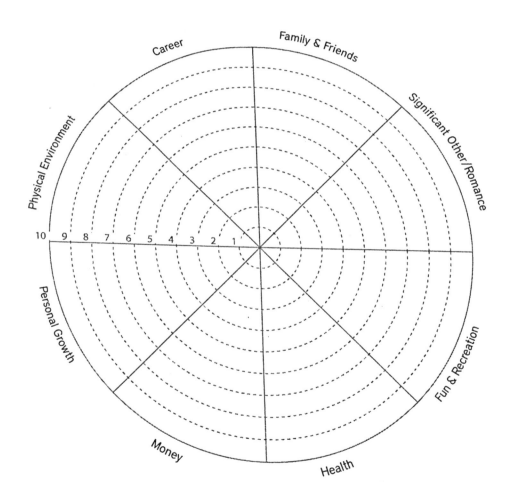

The Lie

⸻

"You will not surely die," the serpent said to the woman. "For God knows that when you eat of it your eyes will be opened, and you will be like God, knowing good and evil."

—Genesis 3:4-5

Have you ever conversed with the tempter? It's not easy to duck his vomit. His tongue quickly spews discontent. The vibration of his voice is a rhythm of bareness and black soot, yet he oozes words of flattery in exchange for your life and mine. Eve was not aware of his death sentence, clearly packaged to entice the eye. He promised gainful wisdom between good and evil, yet deceived at a crossroad to live or die. But wait! Do you care yet? Was Eve expecting, or was she chasing what she expected life to be? I guess it's like asking the difference between love and lust—they both feel good in the moment, but one never satisfies, and one never fails.

Have you figured out who lied to you? Has there been a time in your life when someone you thought had your best interest at heart betrayed you? Where do you think the root of the lie came from, and who is the father of all lies? Think about how the conversation started. John 8:44 teaches us the lesson of a liar:

> You are of your father the devil, and you want to do the desires of your father. He was a murderer from the beginning, and does not stand in the truth because there is no truth in him. Whenever he speaks a lie, he speaks from his own nature, for he is a liar and the father of lies.

Yesterday you should've taken the Wheel Assessment and learned about your strengths and needs. Were there areas where you felt stuck? I can almost guarantee that the areas where the most improvement is needed, is the areas where someone lied to you. Use this time to go back and reflect on a time when someone lied to you in one of the domains. For example, someone said to me, "You will never get married because you are too independent." As a result, unconsciously or consciously, I was stuck in noncommittal relationship and never looked at the root of where that lie came from. Even people with good intentions will put their lies on us based on their experiences—that's why you can't trust experience alone. Despite the good intentions, what is God saying to you? Proverb 31:10: "A wife of noble character who can find? She is worth far more than rubies." Believe what God says about you! You have self-wealth, and your treasures will be found.

Don't Bite Off More Than You Can Chew

⚬⚬⚬

"But I am afraid that as the serpent deceived Eve by his craftiness, your minds will be led astray from the simplicity and purity of devotion to Christ."

—2 Corinthians 11:3

Did Eve really believe that the God who made her in His image would somehow keep something good from her? Do you believe that God is keeping something good from you? Perhaps you're the one holding something back from God? Maybe it's time to get naked with TRUTHS.

Who are you conversing with about living and dying? There's always someone ready to fill in the gaps when you're feeling your most vulnerable. Every aspect of our lives is affected by the fall and the sin it introduced to the world. In our relationships, careers, and all our experiences, we sometimes struggle with our choices. We struggle if we are going to choose pride verses humility, selfishness verse love, especially in those areas of discontent; however, we must make sure we're not disconnected from the truth, or we become like Eve, literally biting off more than we can chew. Outside of God's will for her husband, Eve consumed the nasty fruit of bitterness by listening to the wrong voice.

What is on your mind? What consumes your thoughts daily? A healthy mind has a wealthy life. What are you doing to make sure that your mind is not polluted with deceit? Take time to take inventory of your thought life.

God wants us to live in the authority that He has given us; Eve was given authority until she gave up her position for a lie.

Write down the lies you've told yourself or others. How is the lie damaging your position in the domain areas you listed on Day 18?

Day 21

Are You Hungry?

"You, God, are my God, earnestly I seek you; I thirst for you, my whole being longs for you, in a dry and parched land where there is no water."

—Psalm 63:1

Was it unpardonable vanity or presumption on Eve's part to believe that she could suppress her unfulfilled appetite? Is a forbidden behavior the result of an unmet need? But what was she missing? Was it her starving motivation to know good and evil? Was she trying to seek the peak of self-fulfillment independent from her relationship with God? Eve had a desire to "become more and more what one is, to become everything that one is capable of being," but at what cost? How do we understand our needs so that they don't become bigger than our need for God?

The following is an illustration of Maslow's hierarchy of needs, which gives us insight into his theory of human motivation. What do you think Eve needed? No need can ever be isolated from another need. I believe when we understand our needs, we are less likely to believe the lie of our enemy that tells us that our needs will never be satisfied. "For apart from me, you can do nothing" (John 15:5).

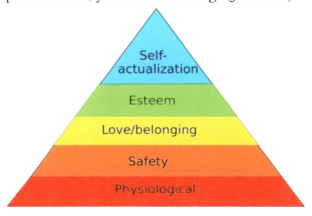

How Do You Make Decisions?

"He who gives an answer before he hears, it is folly and shame to him."

—Proverbs 18:13

Eve had a decision to make, and sometimes it's harder to make a decision if you're not accurately sorting through the truth. Do you have all the facts before you make a decision? I want to share with you the Ladder of Inference that was first put forward by Psychologist Chris Argyris. This is thinking tool that helps us to sift through the process of how we think. It's important to gather the facts when making an informed decision. How we gather information is pivotal to our success and spiritual inheritance. How do you make decisions? Do you gather all the facts before making important decisions? On the next page, we will take a closer look at how Eve made decisions through the Ladder of Inference. Choose to start from the bottom of the ladder and work your way up. I've used Eve as my case study to sift my thinking through the Ladder of Inference. The biblical principles are the facts or evidence that support Eve eating the forbidden fruit, and we will use the Ladder of Inference to guide us through the decision making process. Keep in mind that although this is a very powerful tool, our heavenly Father has the final say.

Reality and Facts

"But God did say, 'you must not eat fruit from the tree that is in the middle of the garden, and you must not touch it, or you will die.'

—Genesis 3:3

Selected Reality

Genesis 3:4–5

What did she select as her reality? You will not certainly die, the serpent said to the woman. For God knows that when you eat from it your eyes will be opened, and you will be like God. Knowing good and evil.

Interpreted Reality

"When the woman saw that the fruit of the tree was good for food and pleasing to the eye, and also desirable for gaining wisdom, she took some and ate it."

—Genesis 3:6

Assumptions

"'Who told you that you were naked?' the Lord God asked. 'Have you eaten from the tree whose fruit I commanded you not to eat?'"

—Genesis 3:11

Conclusions

"So the Lord God banished him from the Garden of Eden to work the ground from which he had been taken."

—Genesis 3:21–23

Beliefs

"Paul argues, 'As in Adam all die, so in Christ all will be made alive.'"

—1 Corinthians 15:22

Actions

When the Lord was walking in the Garden of Eden after Adam and Eve sinned, He came to seek those who had been lost. This loving action is one of God's characteristics that shows that when humankind sinned, He still loved us and had a plan in place for salvation.

"And the Lord God called unto Adam and said unto him, 'Where art thou?' (The first time we hear God was seeking the lost) and he said. 'I heard the sound of you in the garden, and I was afraid, because I was naked, and I hid myself.'"

—Genesis 3:9–10

Too Much on Your Plate?

"Come unto me, all ye that labor and are heavy laden, and I will give you rest."

—Matthew 11:28–29

Too much on your plate won't help you funnel through the process of good decision-making.

I believe if you're not conscious of your appetite and intake, you're headed for a lifestyle of gluttony. The plate I've carried has been spilling over with toxicity for years. I can't say that it represents my full course, but I know I have had my portion, besides that I wasn't meant to serve myself or be a gorger for life. I've watched many women carry too much on their plates, but don't be too hard on yourself if this sounds like you. It took some major setbacks for me to understand that prioritizing what was on my plate and clean eating would help me to live longer.

Listen, take off that cape on the back of your outfit—it's just a façade. Please stop burning both ends of the candle and start setting healthy boundaries for yourself. Remember that too much on anyone's plate will eventually spill over for others to clean up. And when that happens, it makes it harder to differentiate your wants from your needs. Some days I've eaten everything the world puts in front of me. Prayer has been my keeper and my hope for change, but the Word has been my clean eating. God cancels the menu of daily disappointments when He says, "Taste and see that the Lord is good; blessed is the one who takes refuge in him" (Psalm 34:8).

Go into your kitchen and place a few objects on a plate until it's completely covered. Don't discriminate—use whatever you see, such as glasses, dish detergent, pots, pans, and utensils. The plate represents you, and the objects represent your roles and functions in your life. Once you have done that, hold your plate with one hand and see how long you can hold it before objects start falling off. See if you can hold the plate for five minutes.

God desires for us to decipher His voice, so that we are not carrying more than we can handle. Matthew 11:28-29 reminds us that he will give us rest. When was the last time you rested from what you were carrying? Write down how you felt doing this activity. Was this difficult to achieve? What would you have done differently to keep the plate steady?

Are You Playing?

"The righteous person may have many troubles, but the Lord delivers him from them all."

—Psalm 34:19

In my pursuit to satisfy my own appetite, I've raced with thoughts outside of God's will and wrestled with the bittersweetness that dangled in front of me and made me feel anxious. I couldn't get past the noise and distractions. I found shortcuts and let the law of attraction pollute, increase my binges and cravings, offering me lies and deceit. I knew I held the key, but I kept wearing the shackles that bound me. But God knows I'm not good at throwing my own pity party; besides, it would only prove me to be a counterfeit. Instead I'll get naked with truth. The truth is, some days I was praying with fire, and some days I was playing with fire. I was afraid of the shackles that frustrated me, not realizing that frustrations were just a smoke screen of the truth. Your frustrations are spiritual holes that need to be filled with God's word. Meditate on the following scriptures so that you might water the holes of your heart and be filled.

1 Thessalonians 5:15

James 1:19-22

Ephesians 4:26-27

Numbers 21:4-6

You make the choice today. What happens when you pray? How has prayer been a benefit for you and others that you might have prayed for?

Fear or Forward?

———✦———

"So do not fear, for I am with you; do not be dismayed, for I am your God. I will strengthen you and help you; I will uphold you with my righteous right hand."

—Isaiah 41:10

Fear and forward—what an oxymoron, right? And if you think Eve had some troubles making decisions in her truth°… well, it's twenty years later, and I was still trying to move from this place called stuck. There was an urgency to find the bars that kept me caged in this old reflection. The spark of creativity that was smothered with the mundane responsibilities of adult life needed to be set free.

I raced to what I thought was my resolve, except instead of confronting the enemy of my soul, I made friends with fear, and my enemies had become come my "frenemies." Fear was keeping me from revisiting the hollow dungeons of my past, and my future was on the line. It was time to fight to win, but I was ambivalent.

Being ambivalent paralyzes your future and keeps you from change.

In what areas have you been ambivalent? The ambivalent areas of your life keep you straddling the fence, and we all know the pain that is caused if you fall down the middle. We have to choose to move forward.

Draw a straight line below that represents the fence of fear and forward. This following line represents your timeline, write your birth date at the beginning, and the age you want to live to see at the end. In addition to that, write your current age in the middle. Look at your life prior, how does it compare to right now? Write on the timeline what your future self is doing. Do you have time to be ambivalent? I saw this exercise demonstrated differently on a Dr. Phil and Oprah interview. The lessons of fear, forward, urgency, ambivalence, and purpose all remained relevant. This will help you get off of the fence, tear down the invisible barriers that separate you from reaching your creative core, and the best of who God created you to be.

Bleeding Messy

She said to herself, *"If only I could touch his cloak, I will be healed."*

—Matthew 9:21

I revisited one of the places where I had found myself stuck, and although it wasn't there where the paralytic state began, it was a good place to begin prying open the bars of my past. Evening hit, and I rushed from work to make it to my old community college. It was right there; I stopped to take this snapshot of my past.

Please capture this image of the bench with me, because if I lose it, I'm grieved. The Artist is drawing me sitting on the bench waiting for life. I'm hemorrhaging with lost hope, and somehow I can't figure out if it's the lost image, the blood or the lost time that pains me. Never mind, let's just try to snap past this image. The colors are getting too intense to watch, as if the artist dropped her brush and was not able to pick it back up. The canvas is starting to bleed red.

Is your life hemorrhaging?

In a few minutes I'd like for you to sit with God, and envision the leaking areas of your life being made whole. The picture above is a representation of the leaky and messy areas of my life and after painting it I meditated on Philippians 1:6, "For I am certain of this very thing, that he by whom the good work was started in you will make it complete till the day of Jesus Christ."

The Bench

"If we confess our sins, he is faithful and just and will forgive our sins and purify us from all unrighteousness."

—1 John 1:9

It's hard to move forward if you haven't faced the strongholds of your past. This day is so important, and I don't take strongholds lightly because their clawlike grip can be damaging. If the wounds don't heal properly, they can reopen. When the wounds reopen you may almost be deceived into thinking that the clawing grip was far better. I want my beautiful sisters to be unleashed from the clawlike grip through the power of the blood of Jesus. I also want my sisters to understand when the grip took hold and how it became a stronghold in the first place. That's why this day is entitled "The Bench"—we need to park for a while. Strongholds are built on error and falsehood. It is always important to understand your faulty thinking patterns. Those patterns are built over time and can be fueled by your social, biological, psychological, environmental, and spiritual influences. When we accept and receive errors in our life as truth, the grip will begin to form. If these strongholds are a result of faulty thinking, then we can trust these biblical principles and stand on the promises of God. Please right your faulty thinking right next to the scriptures below and compare your thinking to what the Word says:

"(For the weapons of our warfare are not carnal, but mighty through God to the pulling down of strongholds;) Casting down imaginations, and every high thing that exalteth itself against the knowledge of God, and bringing into captivity every thought to the obedience of Christ."

—2 Corinthians 10:4

"For our struggle is not against flesh and blood, but against the rulers, against power, against the spiritual forces of wickedness in the heavenly places."

—Ephesians 6:12

"And be not conformed to this world: but be ye transformed by the renewing of your mind, that ye may prove what is that good, and acceptable, and perfect, will of God."

—Romans 12:2

Is there an error of faulty thinking? Where did it come from? Was it passed down to you from the generation before you? Asses your environment. How does your environment contribute to the faulty thinking? Are you being honest with God? Are you and God engaged in a relationship, or are you just a Cultural Christian? Culture changes constantly, but God doesn't.

The Secret

"For freedom Christ has set you free; stand firm therefore, and do not submit again to the yoke of slavery."

—Galatians 5:1

I couldn't seem to get up from the bench; heck, I was eighteen just waiting on forever to come. My mother pulled up in front of the bench and in her demanding voice said. "Get in!" It was as if the camera clicked and captured me in that moment and I was stuck there. I knew it was the time to shut up, grow up, and kiss innocence good-bye. Her voice was as cold and stiff as the planks I sat on. I slowly got up, and at that moment the secret in my soul was no longer mine. My faulty thinking began.

Is there a secret that's locked in the seat of your soul? If you realize you are hiding behind the secret, it may be keeping you from having the true intimacy that you will experience with Abba Father, our Lord and Savior Jesus Christ.

Pray this with me as you fill in your name.

Today I, _____, surrender this secret to you and release the guilt that keeps my soul caged and my spirit from being free. As I release (fill in the blank) _____ _____, the secret that has kept me in the bondage, I also embrace my freedom. Abba Father, You are concerned about everything that concerns me, and in You there is no secret because You knew me in my mother's womb. Most importantly, I believe that I am Your beloved and that You love me. Thank You for renewing my mind on this day, and I am released from the secret that has entangled me. I am sure of Your love for me in the matchless name of Jesus. You are my Jehovah-Rapha, the Lord, my healer. Amen

Change

"'Come now, and let us reason together,' saith the Lord, 'though your sins be as scarlet they shall be as white as snow; though they be red like crimson shall be as wool.'"

—Isaiah 1:18

It was the glare in her eyes that caged my spirit. I instantly became blind to the intensity of color and started on my new journey of gray. I couldn't release the liquids in my eyes; it was then that I learned I couldn't cry. The bench was streaked with stains; I waited for the rain, but the drought remained my plank of shame. If you would've told me I had purpose, I would've told you were lying. If you would've told me, but you didn't. What I needed was change, and for you to tell me about the intensity of change. Who would break this cycle that seems more intense than change itself? The Transtheoretical Model (Stages of Change), by Prochaska and Diclemente, has six stages and was designed to help smokers through their healing process. Is change your desire? It takes courage to change the way we think and behave. Why would someone want to change a part of themselves when it's easier to revert to old behaviors. We know change won't occur overnight that's why I'm challenging you to 40 days of contemplative activities? Please asses your attitudes, values, and beliefs through this process. Coach yourselves to forward action.

Scream this out loud: …

> MY PURPOSE IS CHANGE IN THE PROCESS!

Stick a note on your mirror, write it on your social media status, or hashtag it. You are in the process of change! Now walk in TRUTHS as you read the six stages below.

The stages of change are:

Pre-contemplation (not yet acknowledging that there is a problem behavior that needs to be changed)

Contemplation (Acknowledging that there is a problem but not yet ready or sure of wanting to make a change)

Preparation/Determination (Getting ready to change)

Action (You have the will to change the behavior)

Maintenance (Maintaining the behavior change)

Relapse (Returning to old behaviors and abandoning the new changes

Where are you in your process?

A New Day of Naked

Job said, "Naked I came from my mother's womb, and naked I will depart." The Lord gave, and Lord be praised.

—Job 1:21

"It's a new day," I sang loudly in my Nina Simone voice. "Okay, pick up that transcript and walk by the bench," I told myself as I got closer to the registrar building. "You can do it."

Finally, I made it inside the college, refusing to take off my jacket. Maybe I was ashamed that my silk blouse would reveal the fear reeking from underneath my arms, or the truth I wasn't ready to confront in my process of change. I stuttered these words: "Please let me speak to an academic advisor. I need to look at my transcript."

What does your transcript of life reflect?

Your old transcript does not reflect your new message, we were created in God's image and in that image we can create. 2 Corinthians 5:17, reminds us "Therefore, if anyone is in Christ, the new creation has come: The old has gone, the new is here! So why are we literally sweating the small stuff? Why are we reeking? It is time for us to Create an affirmation that lipsticks our truth. A young woman named Tiffany told me she lipsticks her affirmations on the mirror to remind her of her truth. Now take a selfie with your lipstick truth.

My Affirmation...........Today my heavenly Father loves me just as I am, even in my nakedness. Today He is clothing me with love, and I am learning to love myself in the boundless nature of His Love.

Job said, "Naked I came from my mother's womb and naked I will depart." The Lord gave, and Lord has taken away; may the Lord be praised. Today, get ready and take on a Job attitude. Praise Him past your circumstance and your past!

How does Job 1:21 relate to your new day? You are getting closer to your core as you take time to write and meditate on these scriptures.

Intimidation

⸺⊶⧓⧓⊷⸺

"'Do not be afraid of them for I am with you and will rescue you,' declares the Lord."

—Jeremiah 1:8

Intimidation met me at my open door, and it was a student who was half my age. Furthermore, why was he so confused by what I was asking him to do? I got so angry and annoyed with him. "Like please, hurry up!" I know we've met before. I'm the bench girl, and your name is Peeping Tom. You looked into my soul and told my secrets. You knew me when I was vulnerable, alone, and scared. Mr. Intimidation, today you will be evicted! Move! You're just a boy; you haven't grown since my last snapshot, and besides, you're standing in front of my open door!

Who is in front of your open door? Please take authority today and visualize yourself pushing through the opening, the barriers, and the people moving out of your way. Call them out because the sweat beneath your arms is not becoming. Intimidation is another smoke screen in front of your promise. Move!

Move!

"I will instruct you and show you the way to go; with My eye on you, I will give counsel."

—Psalm 32:8

I wish for women to embrace their vulnerabilities and stand up to their fears. Behind this door I'm facing the unknown, yet I make speculations of what's going to change, and somehow I'd rather open the door for you than for me. I guess I'm just wired that way. Besides, I really believe that people want to move forward, and people want to change, but ask me how to do that without opening the door? So go ahead, open it. I'll wait. If you won't, then I will.

How do we open the door? Let's thank God in advance for this day and the opportunity that it brings to us. We know that we are empowered today beyond our natural strength, that the strength that we have today is the power to push beyond our limits, obstacles, and barriers! Gratitude will push open your doors today, please make a gratitude list below, give thanks upon the Lord. Put your list on the refrigerator, attach it to your car dashboard, or hang it in your office. Move! "Give thanks to the Lord, call upon his name, and make known his deeds among the people" (Psalm 105:1)

_____

_____

_____

_____

_____

"Then I shall give you rains in their season so that the land will yield its produce and the trees of the field will bear their fruit."

—Leviticus 26:4

The rain clouds were shifting forcing the rain to fall aggressively. I was fishing for my future, ready to step out of the boat called chance. Suddenly I hooked on to something new, my shift. The academic advisor held the infamous transcript and said, "You only have thirty-three credits to complete this degree! But you grades were inconsistent, and I'll start with the A's first." She amused me with a couple of B's, and then BAM! She hit me with an F. It splashed my face like I was drowning. I wanted the weird, crooked grin on her face to stop, just stop!

But in that moment, I got a snapshot. It was from sixth grade, and I heard the voice of little Ms. Abbatelli, a classmate who had been my thorn for three years, say, "You don't belong in our school" and "Get off the playground with my friends." This little girl had held me hostage in the coat room with a number-two pencil for the last time. *Stop!*

It was the color of my skin that she wanted to erase, but before she could, I yelled stop! And that quick I had come out of that snapshot. The academic advisor asked if I was okay, and at that moment the camera in my mind broke. "Stop," I said. "I am more than my transcript!"

It is time to turn the paradigm upside-down, and here's how we will do it.

Stop and say this out loud!

"Today I have unlimited potential. My hopes and dreams are manifesting. Here I am, naked again, but I am forgiven, and my failures don't determine my future."

Today I let go and forgive little Ms. Abbatelli and anyone who has ever threatened my existence. I reject words of rejection, such as, "You don't belong," because I hold my worth to the truth of God's Word! As a result, I will stop looking through the lenses of rejection to measure my self-wealth.

Today I praise God for the new transcript, and my failures have been wiped clean. There is no dead thing operating in my life, and regardless of what has been, I have many opportunities in my future.

Exercise your faith today by voicing your praise! This journey is about writing your new transcript. Be intentional, adjust your prescription, take off your rejection lenses and draw a new pair of glasses below. Write on your lenses how you will excel at your best you. Remember God determines your future, and your future will serve.

The Battle

—∻—

"He said, 'Listen, King Jehoshaphat and all who live in Judah and Jerusalem! This is what the Lord says to you: do not be afraid or discouraged because of this vast army. For the battle is not yours, but God's.'"

—2 Chronicles 20:15

I knew the academic advisor wasn't aware of the battle I had going on in my head, but I had no time to waste on my past. The academic advisor was unengaged and ready for me to get out of her office as she pointed me to the open door. "Turn right and go down the hall, and you can purchase your official transcript," she said. Really? Did I need to officially purchase my original transcript, to move past my past? Although my body felt numb, I could finally move!

Can life make you numb? There are two powerful words that will help you move into your self-wealth: God is! These two words confirm who we are. Because God is, I am. You and I are made in His image. Below write who God is to you; as a result, this will confirm your "I am" in Him!

God is_____ I am_____

God is_____ I am_____

God is_____ I am_____

God is_____ I am_____

God is_____ I am_____

God is_____ I am_____

God is_____ I am_____

God is_____ I am_____

God is_____ I am_____

God is_____ I am_____

God is_____ I am_____

God is_____ I am_____

God is_____ I am_____

Don't Die a Girl

"When He had gone in, He said to them, 'Why make a commotion and weep? The child has not died, but is sleeping.' Taking the child's hand, He said to her, 'Talithakum!'" (which translates from Aramaic to, "Little girl, I say to you, get up!")

—Mark 5:39 and 41.

Although the transcript did not officially transcribe who I was, my attitude was different. I decided who was going to transcribe my future. This was my playground; my creative core was not in the transcript I held, but in the hands that held me daily. No longer was I going to sell my self-worth; I ran quickly for my self-wealth. The night seemed dark, almost like the color of suicide. The rubric that measured me was broken, and the amends I made as I passed by the bench was with the little girl who sat on it—me. I had released what held me back and became naked with truth.

Is there a little girl in you who has died? Or is she sleeping, and can she be healed? Allow the Holy Spirit to restore her to the woman that she was purpose to be.

Little Girl you were successful even back then. You made it through many failed relationships and daily disappointments." Before I could utter another word, I had to set her free. There was nothing else to hold on to. The sun began its kiss, and there was a breakthrough. The snapshot ended when the camera broke. All the images began to get blurred. As I passed the bench, it was no longer there, and neither was the little girl. Everyone who had passed her and rejected her were just broken soul ties. The roots that entangled her had been loosed by forgiveness, redemption, and love. She had birthed what was expected. She claimed her nakedness through the garden of possibilities, and she produced beautifully!

Have you forgiven those who hurt you, and have you forgiven yourself? Write a letter to someone who you have not forgiven and then release him or her. When you do that, you set yourself free. Lastly, write a letter to the little girl in you, and tell her she did it.

Now That You're Naked

"I will praise thee; for I am fearfully and wonderfully made; and marvelous are thy works; and that my soul knoweth right well."

—Psalm 139:14

So now that you're naked, it's time for conception to take place. Are you concerned about your body flaws or imperfections? Are you still worried about that one thing that you haven't perfected according to the measures of this world? Please stand in front of a mirror to see the beauty of God's creation and take notice, you, my dear are his perfect imperfection. Your self-wealth is at the core and is getting fat. You are pregnant with the seed of truth in you. God is birthing something in you, and while you are waiting, He wants to whisper His plan for your delivery.

I want you to start packing the things you will need for the delivery room. For example, you are going to have to pack prayer because it's the communication that will help you birth your promise. Prayer is your umbilical cord, God is breathing new life into you today.

Are you ready? The labor pains are intense, but sooner or later, it will be your time to push! Make sure you pack your bag with the right stuff.

You've shut the door and said No to what's been stopping you from your delivery process. Position your midwives to be on watch because they will stand in the gap while you are pushing. They will keep those people out of the labor room who don't belong. My cousin Robin would do this "NAKED NO" activity with me whenever we felt the challenge to push to our next level. We would stand a few inches in front of each other practicing the power of the word No. "Are you ready to push?" I would ask. Then say No! Say no as often as you need to until something breaks. "NO!" She would yell! "Louder you don't believe it!" "NOOOOOOOO!" Yes, that's it! I laughed every time we did this activity, although she was in the military she didn't mind practicing this command with me because she understood what it meant to get your orders for a mission.

"Naked No" will give you the power to find your voice and use your voice when other voices become the barrier to your breakthrough. Find your midwife, stand in front of her and ask her to help you say No to everything that keeps you from trusting! Push in your nakedness until you feel a breakthrough!

I'm Pregnant and Scared!

"When a woman is giving birth, she has sorrow because her hour has come, but when she has delivered the baby, she no longer remembers the anguish, for joy that a human being has been born into the world."

—John 16:21

I know throwing a note down the steps that read "I'm pregnant" was not the way to break the news to my dear mother when I was nineteen, but looking back, I was so immature. I was so afraid to face my reality and my enemies, and guilt, shame, and defeat hovered over me, gripping my tongue. I couldn't speak.

The note spiraled down like a reckless plane. My mother was sitting in a chair near the bottom of the steps, and as she picked up the note, she said, "This isn't funny." Well, I wasn't laughing, and the look in her eyes told me that my plane had just crashed.

Have you ever done the very thing you said you weren't going to do? I have, many times over in pursuing this perfect life that didn't exist, and it was during the times I said, "Oh, I'd never..." that I did! Forget about never, or it will become your default. Some people spend their entire lives focusing on never, and the very thing that was never has become. I love focusing on things that are forever, things that will last and things that eradicate the very limits of never. "I will never" doesn't measure where I am going, but forever does.

Ponder on this: What are the things that will become forever? They will eliminate never.

It's Time

"To every thing there is a season, and a time to every purpose under the heaven: A time to be born, and a time to die; a time to plant, and a time to pluck up that which is planted."

—Ecclesiastics 3:1-2

How do you know when it's time? Maybe time will fly, like the flying note that was delivered to my mother when I told her I was pregnant? How immature was that?

Looking back, I realize that I became a parent before I was probably ready. I had so many unmet needs in my life. I was still trying to progress through some of my basic needs, and now there was going to be someone who needed me. Despite my lack of readiness, being pregnant felt somehow bittersweet—I was confused and secretly excited too. Nonetheless, this was a very challenging time, and I knew my parents had different expectations for me. I told my mom I was pregnant but was terrified to tell my dad. Hey dad, I'm pregnant, yeah right! I wanted my mother to make that announcement.

Two weeks went by, and my mom eventually told him. I will never forget the sound of the door as he opened my bedroom door. I still remember the blue room that felt as cold as the events that led to my dad opening my door. He said, "What's this I hear? You're pregnant?" I nodded my head yes, and silence filled the room. A few seconds felt like eternity. And then he said, "Well°… I think you're going to be a great mom."

Are you still waiting for someone to speak words of power over you? How do you think it would have changed the trajectory of your life? Write down what you want to hear in the space below, and repeat the words out loud to yourself.

My Father's Voice

"So you have not received a spirit that makes you fearful slaves. Instead you received God's spirit when he adopted you as his own children now we call him Abba Father."

—Romans 8:15

Ideally, all girls want to hear the approval of their fathers. My father's words pierced my soul and revived my spirit. A father's words can hold so much weight. It's a voice that we yearn to hear; it gives us strength when we're weak and lights up a dark path.

Whether your father is present or absent, he's an eternal barometer that seems to measure your worth. Even if your biological father is absent, you always have a heavenly Father who seeks your love and waits to speak life into your circumstances.

Are you listening?

Today take a prayer-walk, but before you leave, write down what you want to say to God. Make sure you make this prayer walk about your active communication between you and God. I know it can be a struggle to hear the voice of God sometimes, but God is still speaking. Listen through your five senses and write down everything that God has spoken to you on your walk.

Your Core

<hr>

"Abide in Me, and I in you. As the branch cannot bear fruit of itself unless it abides in the vine, so neither can you unless you abide in Me."

— John 15:4

Does a pregnancy out of wedlock still bring a promise? "And we know that all things work together to them who are called according to His promise" (Romans 8:23).

By no means am I promoting unplanned pregnancies, or pregnancies out of divine matrimony—our families and communities have suffered too long. However, God's grace has been the umbilical cord to our promise. Besides, who really wants to do this alone? It's crucial to seek wisdom and understanding so that the external and internal pressures don't abort the plans that God has for us.

As a woman who had a child out of wedlock, I understand the ridicule that one might face and the shame and guilt depending on your cultural values and beliefs. God desires for His daughters to enjoy the pleasures of sex, and family, both can be fulfilling and whole, especially when created within the confines of marriage. Make a decision today, receive the best that God has for you, and walk unashamed in your nakedness.

Don't forget to check your vision, Adam and Eve's perception was off. Adam and Eve saw that they were naked and became afraid.

> Then the eyes of both were opened, and they knew that they were naked. And they sewed fig leaves together and made themselves loincloths. And they heard the sound of the Lord God waiting in the garden in the midst of the cool of the day, and the man and his wife hid themselves from the presence of the Lord God among the trees of the garden. But the Lord God called to the man and said to him.

"Where are you? And he said, I heard the sound of you in the garden and I was afraid, because I was naked, and I hid myself. (Genesis 3:7–10)

Why is it so important to get to the core of who you are created to be? The Word of God reveals to us that the man and woman became afraid and covered themselves and their nakedness. It wasn't seeing evil that made them feel ashamed; tasting and eating off the wrong vine is what left them with feelings of shamefulness. I think fig leaves are seriously a cheap way to be fashion forward even in that time. However, when we notice that we have digested the cheap things of this life, it's easy to look for cheap ways to cover our spiritual ills, which is not spiritually flattering or healthy to our souls.

Even after Adam and Eve covered themselves, they still hid. We do this often; we hide behind superficial things away from who we are at our creative cores. Our creative cores are intertwined into the master creator's plan for us; it's as if we have a spiritual umbilical cord that leads to complete godly success. This kind of success changes the atmospheric presence wherever we go. It is a place of spiritual abundance manifested here on earth. It is your self-wealth.

Your self-wealth comes from your core. It is your creative gift, and it's your responsibility to birth that gift into the world. You are called to nurture and care for your gift by taking action. You are responsible for caring for your core: its your gift and self-wealth. You have completed exercises to strengthen your core; it will bring you to a place where you live from the freedom of your self-wealth. How do you perceive where you are right now, in this moment? Whatever you receive is what you perceive. Are you living or dying?

Your Core

"Daughters of Jerusalem I charge you do not arouse or awaken love until it so desires."

—Song of Solomon 8:4

Babies don't recognize their nakedness and are notorious for trying to pull off all their clothes. They will run around naked in front of strangers, without a single thought that it may be inappropriate. They have not eaten off the tree of knowledge that has given them insight into the things that we know can be harmful, such as guilt and shame. To run naked is freeing for a child who doesn't care what you and I think, and the idea of removing layers of guilt and shame is foreign at that stage of development.

It is at the core of innocence that we take risks and humbly create opportunities with a childlike faith. We run for our freedom in nakedness, knowing that we will receive His naked love. The abundance of God's love is what clothes us and takes us from a place where the bitter fruit in our lives survives and is replace with our spiritual fruit. Galatians 5:22–23 describes love, joy, forbearance, kindness, goodness, faithfulness, gentleness, and self-control. How much can you show us your love by clothing us in our nakedness and giving us the clothes of righteousness? Righteousness underserved that you justified for us at the cross. Thank you for the freedom of that love, which helps us chase You, who is the Master Creator at the creative core where the TRUTHS lies within us. Where our thinking is renewed under the Holy Spirit, and with our first parents Adam and Eve you continue to ask, "Where art thou?" Do you think God didn't know where Adam was? A question we must ask ourselves from time to time is "_____ (your name), where art thou? Am I where I'm supposed to be, or am I in hiding?" "Where are thou?" is a question that makes searching that creative core urgent because we want to be aligned with the will of God.

Nakedness is not the sin, but a fallen perception of nakedness is associated with shame and guilt, which brings us into the mental anguish that God was trying to spare Adam and Eve from in the garden. God's provision, even after the shame is a clear indicator of how much He loves us. Later in the chapter readings of Genesis, we notice that the nature of the clothing provided by God was made from the skin of an animal. I would conclude that the death of the innocent animal was sufficient to cover the shame of sin, yet insufficient to atone for the guilt, because Adam and Eve were banned from the garden.

We do not have to live in the shame and guilt of our nakedness. Jesus Christ has atoned for the guilt and shame in our place. We just have to be able to discover this at the core, and we do so by finding that place of stillness. It is the at the core of our being that we find that freedom.

Find a quiet place and meditate on Ezekiel 16:4–14 below. Please read it aloud, and as you do, envision your places of vulnerability. How does the passage speak to your core?

> As for your nativity, on the day you were born your naval cord was not cut, nor were you washed in water to cleanse you: your were not rubbed with salt nor wrapped in swaddling cloths. No eye pitied you, to do any of these things for you, to have compassion on you; but you were thrown out into the open field, when you yourself were loathed on the day you were born.
>
> And when I passed by you and saw you struggling in your own blood, I said to you in your blood, 'Live!' Yes, I said to you in your blood, 'Live!' I made you thrive like a plant in the field; and you grew, matured, and became very beautiful. Your breasts were formed, your hair grew; but you were naked and bare. When I passed by you again and looked upon you, indeed your time was the time of love; so I spread My wing over you and covered your nakedness. Yes, I swore an oath to you and entered into an oath.
>
> Then I washed you in water; yes, I thoroughly washed off your blood, and I anointed you with oil. I clothed you with fine linen and covered you with silk. I adorned you with ornaments, put bracelets on your wrists, and a chain on your neck. And I put a jewel in your nose, earrings in your ears, and a beautiful crown your head. Thus you were adorned with gold and silver, and your clothing was of fine linen, silk, and embroidered cloth. You ate pastry of fine flower, honey, and oil. You were exceedingly beautiful and succeeded to royalty. Your fame went out among the nations because of your beauty, for it was perfect through My splendor which I had bestowed on you," says the Lord God.

This passage takes me to the center of my Father's love, coloring the center of my core. Being naked is the intention to be unintentional.

To flow from the sap of wealth that exudes the innocence of our true nature is our core. There is an Eden hidden in our souls that groans for a greater love. In this place of Eden, we have a decision to make on how we want to receive that greater love. Because greater is He who is in us than He who is in the world. That decision is made daily. I pray that your decisions have not been misguided on this forty-day journey by untruth or distractions. However, we know that our God is sovereign and will makes prolific provisions for us. I hope that the opinion that you have about yourself is the transition and transformation needed to find your self-wealth. I hope that you understand that it is tied to your umbilical cord, and is connected from your center, your core of who God created you to be. He who loves you knew you before you were in your mother's womb. Lastly, as you step into your next level of victory, remember that you will lead from your creative core with assurance that you will birth the promises of God through the connectivity you have with Him in your nakedness. Don't worry about your nakedness as you seek a greater need for Him—He will clothe you in His righteousness and cultivate you to Activate Right Thinking (ART), as we know that on this day all things have worked for our good.

How have you created new ART in your life? Please create a vision board of what that looks like and make that your daily reminder of this forty day journey, and hopefully you will have a creative transformation that will come from your core. I hope this leading from your creative core will take you to places that will bring you in front of greatness! I challenge you to color outside the lines of life and allow the Master Creator to paint your destiny!

You do not have to be an artist; you just have to do ART and God will complete your canvas. Now I want you to take your position. Take a deep breath! As you hear yourself breathing, close your eyes and begin to think about ways you will release gratitude on your journey. The heart of gratitude eliminates the forces that keep us from feeling like we are not enough. Today I celebrate you for taking this forty-day contemplative journey with me. I pray that chains have been broken and that you will create newness where you once saw limits and distractions in your life. I pray that love finds you because you attract what you are. I pray hearts are healed because you have a new identity in the one who heals. I hope for you to release every gift that God has given to you because the world needs you, and it starts with being naked, stripping to the core, and finding that less is more.

About the Author

Life muse Dena Billups is a professional trainer and certified life coach, ministry leader, writer-artist, mother, and wife. Before pursuing her own passions full time, she was an education development specialist who trained a child-welfare workforce throughout New Jersey. In her twenty years as a child-welfare leader, she served vulnerable communities, empowering women and children.

She is the founder of ART of Training and Development, LLC, and partners with churches, nonprofits and educational institutes to offer opportunities where personal growth and self-wealth is more than desirable.

She received her master's in human services from Lincoln University and is on a mission to coach people to soar and reach their creative cores. More importantly, she inspires others to live intentionally in the love of self and others. It is her mission to speak truth and inspire others toward creative stillness.

About the Book

This book will become your daily companion as you use the reflective and creative practices to discover who you are at the core. This book gives people who have dismissed the idea of being creative a second chance. Most of us were robbed of our creativity when we were told to color inside the lines. *Naked* reminds us that we are made in the image of God, and He is the master creator. You will soar as you make a choice to doodle your thoughts, engage in the literature and poetic writings, and complete meditative activities. The number forty was used several times throughout the Bible as a testing time and, as a result, change occurred.

Naked has forty days of authentic truth telling, and no matter where you are in the process of change, you'll never have to remain stuck when you do ART (Activate Right Thinking). *Naked* is a book where biblical principles meet creative practices inspiring you to push toward your creative core and operate from your self-wealth.